My
First Book of

SPANiSH

BUSHEL
& PECK
BOOKS

Text copyright © 2023 by Tony Pesqueira

Published by Bushel & Peck Books, a family-run publishing house in Fresno, California,
that believes in uplifting children with the highest standards of art, music, literature, and
ideas. Find beautiful books for gifted young minds at www.bushelandpeckbooks.com.

Type set in Providence Sans, Learning Curve, Halewyn, and Chelsea Pro
Artwork licensed from Shutterstock.com.

Bushel & Peck Books is dedicated to fighting illiteracy all over the world. For every
book we sell, we donate one to a child in need—book for book. To nominate a school or
organization to receive free books, please visit www.bushelandpeckbooks.com.

LCCN: 2023934698
ISBN: 978-1-63819-153-7

First Edition

Printed in China

1 3 5 7 9 10 8 6 4 2

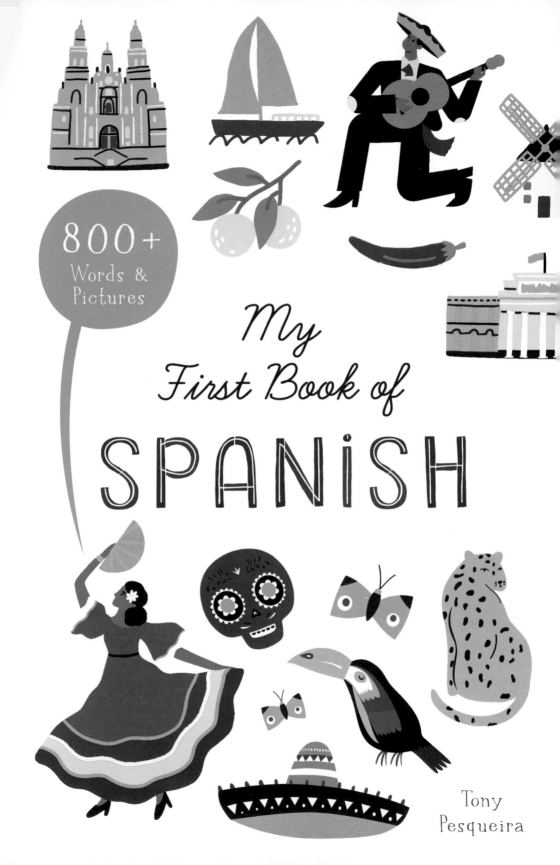

800+
Words &
Pictures

My
First Book of
SPANISH

Tony
Pesqueira

Contents

Good morning!

¡Buenos días!

SPANISH
BASICS

INTRODUCTION

¡Hola! And welcome to *My First Book of Spanish!* The Spanish language is culturally rich and beautiful, and I hope that this book is a helpful starting point as you begin your own Spanish journey. Because this is a beginner's book, I have intentionally kept explanations simple. My goal is to expose first-time learners to the Spanish language without overwhelming their experience with the nuances of Spanish grammar. As such, think of this book as a first look at what I hope will become a continuous adventure of lifetime learning.

¡Suerte!

—Tony Pesqueira

Pronunciation

HOW TO PRONOUNCE EACH LETTER

	HOW TO SAY THE NAME OF THE LETTER	SIMILAR TO ENGLISH SOUND IN:	SPANISH EXAMPLES
a	ah	apple	árbol
b	beh	ball	balón
c	seh	call or cellphone	casa, cerebro
d	deh	*th* sound in though	dedo
e	eh	elephant	elefante
f	efeh	far	fortalecer
g	heh	"H" in Harry or "G" in grand	generación, gato
h	ache	silent "H," like in dough	humildad
i	ee	ski	imposible
j	hota	"H" in Harry	joya
k	kah	kite	kilo
l	ele	love, or "Y" in your if it is a double "L"	lavadora, llorar
m	eme	mom	mamá
n	ene	name	nombre
o	oh	oval	óvalo
p	peh	party	padre

q	coo	**"C" in cool** When you see a "qu" together, the "u" is silent	querido
r	erre	**roll**	ratón
s	esse	**some**	sapo
t	teh	**tie**	telescopio
u	oo	**moose**	utensilio
v	veh	**velvet** (Make the "v" sound lighter for more accurate pronunciation)	vaca
w	doh bleh oo	**waffle**	taiwanés
x	ehkees	**six**	exactamente
y	ee gree eh ga	**yellow**	yugo
z	sehta	**so** (No "Z" sound! It's like an "S" in English)	zapato

UNIQUE LETTERS IN SPANISH

	SIMILAR TO ENGLISH SOUND IN:	SPANISH EXAMPLES
ch	charcoal	¡Qué chido!
ll	your	llorar
ñ	Kenya	caño
rr	**territorial** (When you see two "r"s next to each other in Spanish, try to roll your "r"s by saying ehhhh and lightly touching the tip of your tongue to the space just above and behind your top front teeth)	amarrar

Gender

An important part of the Spanish language is the gender of nouns. There are both masculine and feminine nouns. A noun's gender can determine how other parts of speech are written or pronounced. For example:

La casa es pequeña.

The house is small.

vs.

El libro es pequeño.

The book is small.

Did you notice how the words changed? Look at the spelling for *pequeño* vs. *pequeña*: it's different when the object it's describing (the house vs. the book) is a masculine noun or a feminine one.

This is why, when learning Spanish, it is important to not simply learn nouns but also learn the gender of the nouns.

EL VS. LA

The main way to tell if a noun is feminine or masculine is

whether *el* or *la* is used with the noun. *El* and *la* both mean the English word "the," but in Spanish, they also indicate the gender of the noun they are modifying. For example, the Spanish word for "house" is *casa*. However, *casa* is a feminine noun in Spanish, so to say "the house," you say *la casa*.

el = "the" (for masculine nouns)
la = "the" (for feminine nouns)

There are some words that start with "a," like *agua* or *área*, that are feminine but have *el* in front of the word instead of *la*, so it becomes *el agua* and *el área*. These words, however, remain feminine, even though they start with *el*. So instead of *la agua*, or *la área*, we say *el agua* and *el área* in a much smoother way. There is a tricky aspect to these types of words when they become plural, but we'll talk about that soon.

El is used for some feminine nouns that start with an "a," but not all.
Unfortunately, as with any language, there are exceptions to this rule.

To make nouns plural, you need to see if the noun is masculine or feminine. If the noun is masculine, like *el libro*, to make it plural, you convert *el* to *los* and then add an *s* to *libro* to make *los libros*. If the noun is feminine, like *la casa*, to make it plural, you convert *la* to *las* and add an *s* to *casa* to make *las casas*.

el -> los (for masculine plural nouns)
la -> las (for feminine plural nouns)

Remember when we talked about the tricky feminine nouns

that use el instead of *la*? The tricky part with these nouns is that when they become plural, they revert to their feminine form. We say *el agua* and *el área*, but when these nouns become plural, they become *las aguas* and *las áreas*. Whether singular or plural, these nouns remain feminine despite these unique characteristics. Pretty crazy, right? *¡Qué loco!*

> **Feminine nouns that start with "a" and use *el* when singular use the feminine *las* instead when plural.**

WHAT YOU'LL SEE IN THIS BOOK

Throughout this book, the definite articles *el* and *la* for singular masculine and feminine nouns, and *los* and *las* for plural masculine and feminine nouns, have been included. The articles will appear before each noun so that you can learn the article along with the noun itself!

VOCABULARY

Look for the following tools to help you get the most out of this section:

 Example sentences: See vocabulary in context!

 Language tips: Get extra insight about the meaning or usage of certain words.

 Culture cues: Learn to love the many Spanish cultures alongside the language!

Greetings

Hello, I'm Tony.
Hola, me llamo Tony.

hello /
good day
buenos días

good
afternoon
buenas tardes

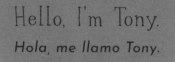

good evening
buenas tardes

good night
buenas noches

 La tarde is often used to refer to both the afternoon and the evening, but you generally won't hear *buenas noches* ("good night") until around 5 pm and after.

● It's nice to meet you. I'm Julie.
Es un placer conocerte. Me llamo Julie.

nice to meet you

es un placer conocerte

goodbye

adiós

I look forward to working with you.

estoy emocionado de poder trabajar contigo.

I am _____.

Yo soy _____.

Courtesy

please
por favor

thanks
gracias
thank you very much
muchas gracias

you're welcome
de nada

excuse me

con permiso

In Spanish you can use *usted* or *tú* to address someone. Generally, it is considered polite to use *usted* with someone you just met.

I'm sorry

lo siento

really?

¿de veras?

no

no

that's right

es verdad

yes

sí

People

person
la persona

baby
el bebé

toddler
el niño

child
el niño

Notice that *el niño* can be used to mean, "boy", "toddler," and "child."

woman
la mujer

girl
la niña

adult
el adulto

man
el hombre

boy
el niño / el chico / el muchacho

She has a little brother.

Ella tiene un hermano menor.

people
*la gente /
las personas*

male
el hombre

female
la mujer

friendly
amigable

friend
el amigo

21

Personal Pronouns

HELLO
MY NAME IS

Sra. Garcia

name
el nombre

Mr.
el señor

Mrs.
la señora

Ms.
la señorita

I
yo

me
yo / mí

you
usted / tú

your
su / tu

She is Mrs. So-and-So.
Ella es la Señora Fulana de Tal.

everybody
todos

they
ellos / ellas

we / us
nosotros / nosotras

them
ellos / ellas

our
nuestros / nuestras

their
sus

she
ella

he
él

his
su / sus

her
su / sus

Land

land
la tierra

mountain range
la sierra

the world
el mundo

geography
la geografía

scenery / landscape
el paisaje

plain
la llanura

Water

ocean
el océano

water
el agua

waterfall
la cascada

sand
la arena

beach
la playa

sea
el mar

coast
la costa

lake
el lago

river
el río

Gulf of Mexico
El Golfo de México

island
la isla

Caribbean Sea
El Mar Caribe

Amazon River
El Río Amazonas

Pacific Ocean
El Océano Pacífico

Atlantic Ocean
El Océano Atlántico

Body

body
el cuerpo

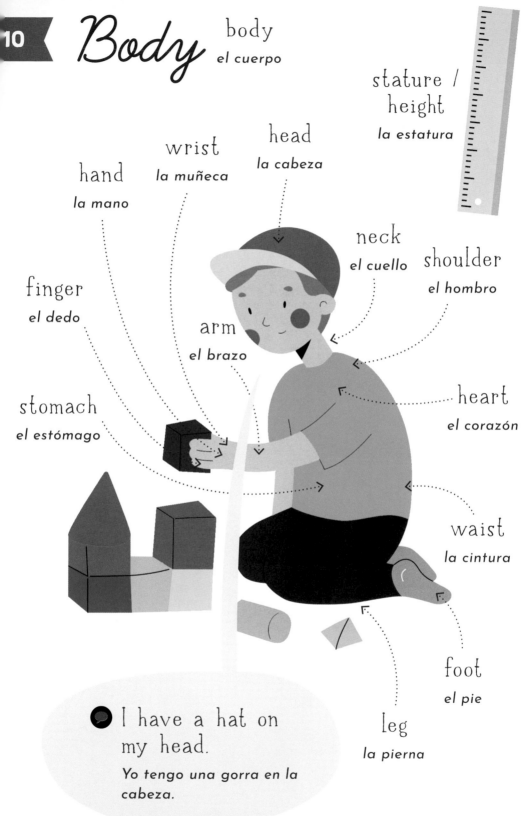

stature /
height
la estatura

wrist
la muñeca

head
la cabeza

hand
la mano

neck
el cuello

shoulder
el hombro

finger
el dedo

arm
el brazo

heart
el corazón

stomach
el estómago

waist
la cintura

foot
el pie

leg
la pierna

💬 I have a hat on
my head.
Yo tengo una gorra en la cabeza.

29

Clothing

We are wearing fashionable clothes.

Llevamos ropa de moda.

clothing
la ropa

to wear
llevar

necktie
la corbata

suit
el traje

dress
el vestido

pants
los pantalones

coat
el abrigo

shoe
el zapato

hat
la gorra / el gorro / el sombrero

raincoat
el impermeable

T-shirt
la camiseta

shirt
la camisa

sock
el calcetín

skirt
la falda

Colors

color

el color

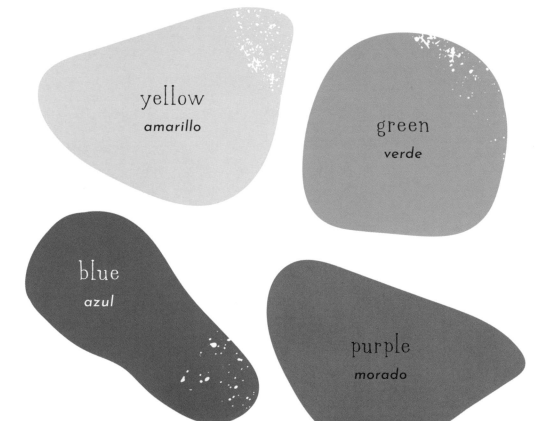

red

rojo

orange

anaranjado

yellow

amarillo

green

verde

blue

azul

purple

morado

The dog is black.

El perro es negro.

white
blanco

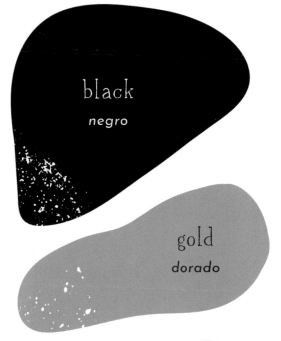

black
negro

gray
gris

gold
dorado

silver
plateado

brown
café

pink
rosado

Opposites

small
pequeño / chico

big
grande

heavy
pesado

light
ligero / liviano

hot
caliente

cold
frío

tall
alto

short
bajo / bajito

*If you turn an "o" to "ito," like when *bajo* becomes *bajito*, the "ito" adds an emphasis to a word meaning that it's even smaller. *Bajo* is short, and *bajito* is very short!

full
lleno

empty
vacío

dirty
sucio

clean
limpio

Shapes

circle
el círculo

square
el cuadrado

rectangle
el rectángulo

triangle
el triángulo

hexagon
el hexágono

pentagon
el pentágono

octagon
el octágono

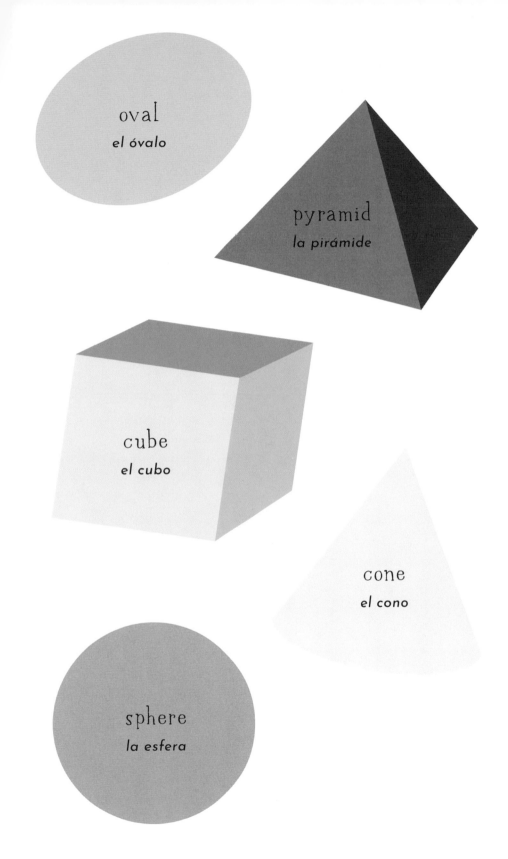

oval
el óvalo

pyramid
la pirámide

cube
el cubo

cone
el cono

sphere
la esfera

My Family

grandma
la abuela

grandpa
el abuelo

mom
la mamá

dad
el papá

parents
los padres

son
el hijo

YOU

daughter
la hija

She has a little brother.
Ella tiene un hermano menor.

family
la familia

uncle
el tío

aunt
la tía

sisters
las hermanas

brothers
los hermanos

big
sister
*la hermana
mayor*

little
sister
*la hermana
menor*

big
brother
*el hermano
mayor*

little
brother
*el hermano
menor*

Directions

directions
las direcciones

map
el mapa

north
el norte

compass
la brújula

west
el oeste

east
el este

near /
close
cerca

south
el sur

far / distant

lejos

Space

planet
el planeta

space
el espacio

universe
el universo

star
la estrella

comet
el cometa

The universe is enormous.
El universo es enorme.

sun
el sol

day
el día

astronaut
el astronauta

air
el aire

sky
el cielo

moon
la luna

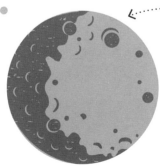

full moon
la luna llena

Weather

weather
el clima / el tiempo

a beautiful day
un día hermoso

cloud
la nube

lightning
el rayo

thunder
el trueno

storm
la tormenta

snow
la nieve

humid
húmedo

hail
el granizo

hurricane
el huracán

tornado
el tornado

rainbow
el arcoíris

rain
la lluvia

wind
el viento

Plants

plants
las plantas

I love to visit the forest.

Me encanta ir al bosque.

tree
el árbol

woods / grove
el bosque

bush
el arbusto

grass
el pasto

forest
el bosque

citrus
el cítrico

leaf
la hoja

marigolds
las caléndulas

trunk
el tronco

flower
la flor

pot
la maceta

greenhouse
el invernadero

rose
la rosa

herbs
las hierbas

47

Animals

animal
el animal

cow
la vaca

cat
el gato

pig
el cerdo

dog
el perro

monkey
*el mono /
el chango*

deer
el venado

fox
el zorro

alligator
el caimán

bear
el oso

polar bear
el oso polar

panda
*el panda
/ el oso
panda*

penguin
el pingüino

elephant
el elefante

lion
el león

49

bird
el pájaro

crane
la grulla

sparrow
el gorrión

chicken
la gallina

crow
el cuervo

insect
el insecto

bee
la abeja

butterfly
la mariposa

salmon
el salmón

frog
la rana

carp
la carpa

tuna
el atún

turtle
la tortuga

snake
*la serpiente / la víbora
/ la culebra*

Seasons

the four seasons
las cuatro estaciones

season
la estación

spring
la primavera

summer
el verano

autumn
el otoño

winter
el invierno

Summer is my favorite season.

El verano es mi estación preferida.

year
el año

calendar
el calendario

this year
este año

last year
el año pasado

next year
el próximo año

every year
cada año

Months

What month is it?
¿En qué mes estamos?

month
el mes

January
enero

February
febrero

March
marzo

April
abril

May
mayo

June
junio

this
month
este mes

next
month
*el próximo
mes*

last
month
*el mes
pasado*

every
month
cada mes

July
julio

August
agosto

September
septiembre

October
octubre

November
noviembre

December
diciembre

Days of the Week

days of the week
los días de la semana

week
la semana

this week
esta semana

next week
la semana próxima

every week
cada semana

last week
la semana pasada

weekday
el día de entre semana

workday
el día laborable / la jornada

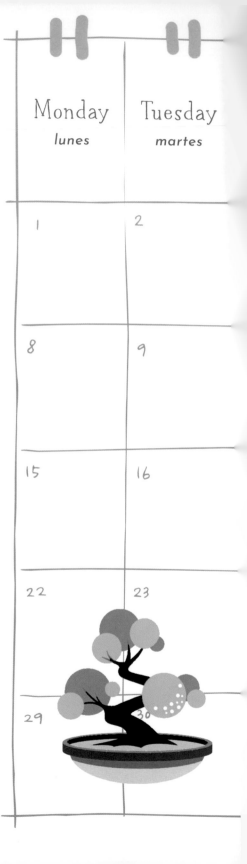

Monday *lunes*	Tuesday *martes*
1	2
8	9
15	16
22	23
29	30

Time

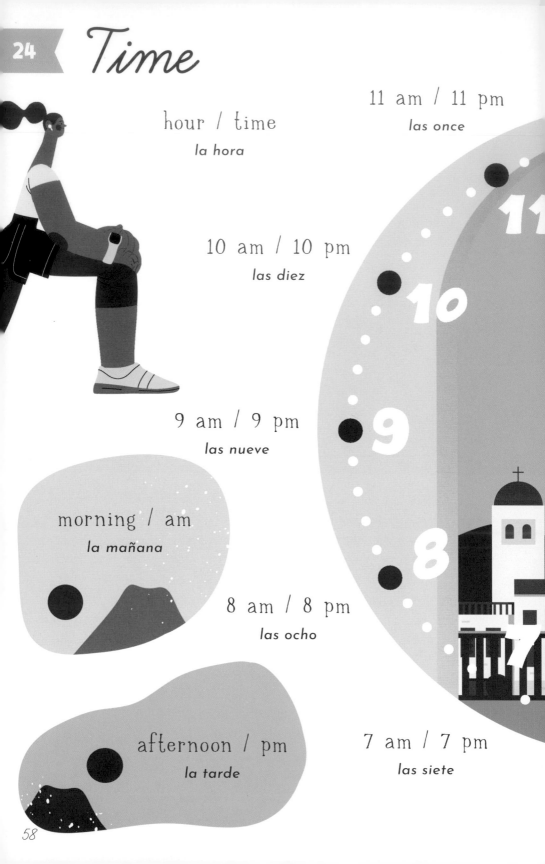

hour / time
la hora

11 am / 11 pm
las once

10 am / 10 pm
las diez

9 am / 9 pm
las nueve

morning / am
la mañana

8 am / 8 pm
las ocho

afternoon / pm
la tarde

7 am / 7 pm
las siete

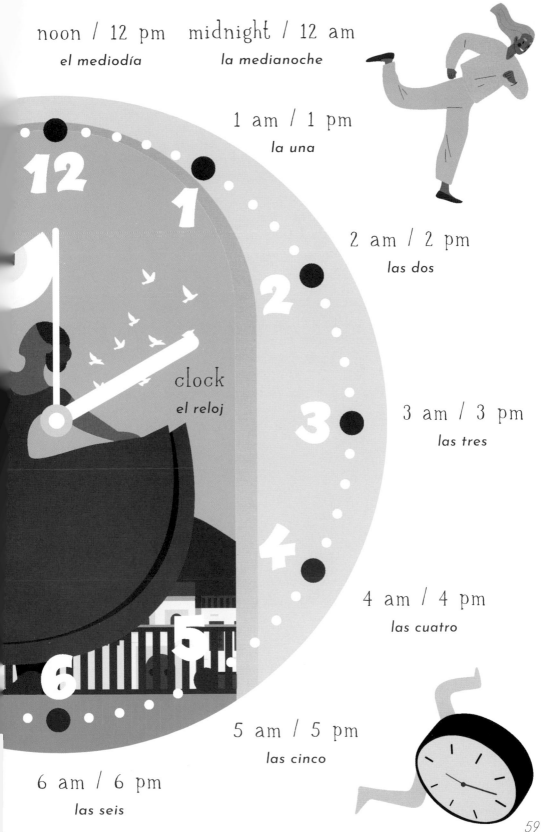

noon / 12 pm
el mediodía

midnight / 12 am
la medianoche

1 am / 1 pm
la una

2 am / 2 pm
las dos

3 am / 3 pm
las tres

4 am / 4 pm
las cuatro

5 am / 5 pm
las cinco

6 am / 6 pm
las seis

clock
el reloj

59

25

Time of Day

now
ahora / ahorita

morning
la mañana

noon / midday
el mediodía

evening
la tarde

evening / night
la noche

night
la noche

midnight
la medianoche

💬 I am going to the doctor at noon.

Voy a ir al doctor al mediodía.

What time is it?

¿Qué hora es? / ¿Qué horas son?

hourglass

el reloj de arena

yesterday

ayer

today

hoy

tomorrow

mañana

every day

cada día

every night

cada noche

every morning

cada mañana

sometimes

a veces

61

26

Countries

parliament
el parlamento

Senate
el senado

country
el país

prime
minister
*el primer ministro /
la primer ministro*

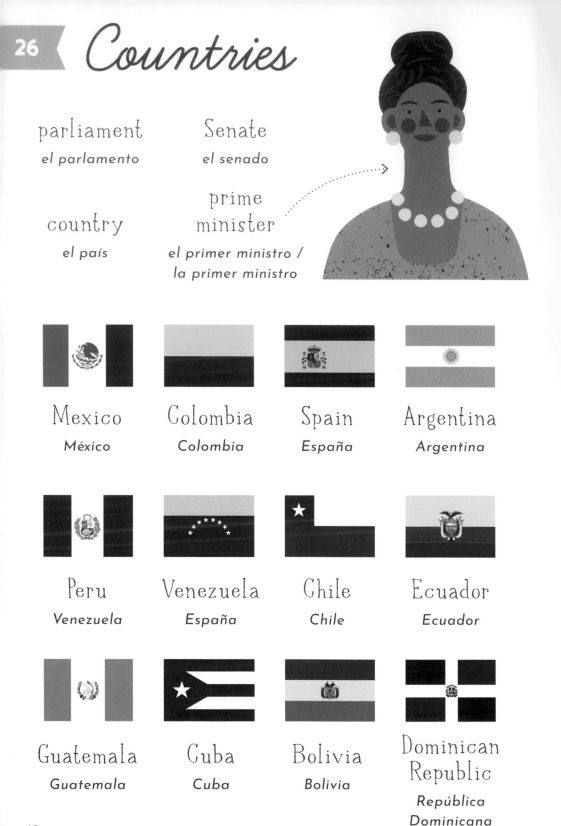

Mexico
México

Colombia
Colombia

Spain
España

Argentina
Argentina

Peru
Venezuela

Venezuela
España

Chile
Chile

Ecuador
Ecuador

Guatemala
Guatemala

Cuba
Cuba

Bolivia
Bolivia

Dominican
Republic
*República
Dominicana*

● You want to
visit Mexico.

*Tú quieres visitar
México.*

← ······· president

*el presidente /
la presidenta*

Honduras
Honduras

Paraguay
Paraguay

El Salvador
El Salvador

Nicaragua
Nicaragua

Costa Rica
Costa Rica

Panama
Panamá

Uruguay
Uruguay

Puerto Rico
Puerto Rico

Equatorial Guinea
*Guinea
Ecuatorial*

 Throughout the world, nearly 500 million
people speak Spanish as their native
language. It's a great one to learn!

27

Urban and Rural

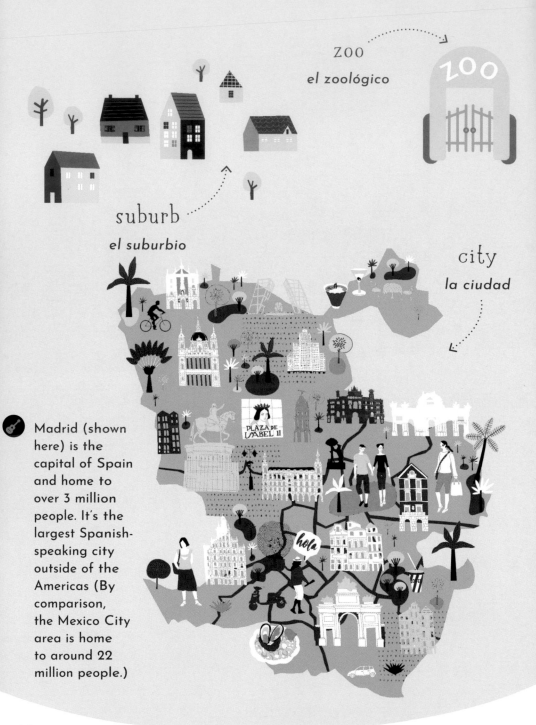

zoo
el zoológico

ZOO

suburb

el suburbio

city

la ciudad

PLAZA DE L'ABEL II

hola

Madrid (shown here) is the capital of Spain and home to over 3 million people. It's the largest Spanish-speaking city outside of the Americas (By comparison, the Mexico City area is home to around 22 million people.)

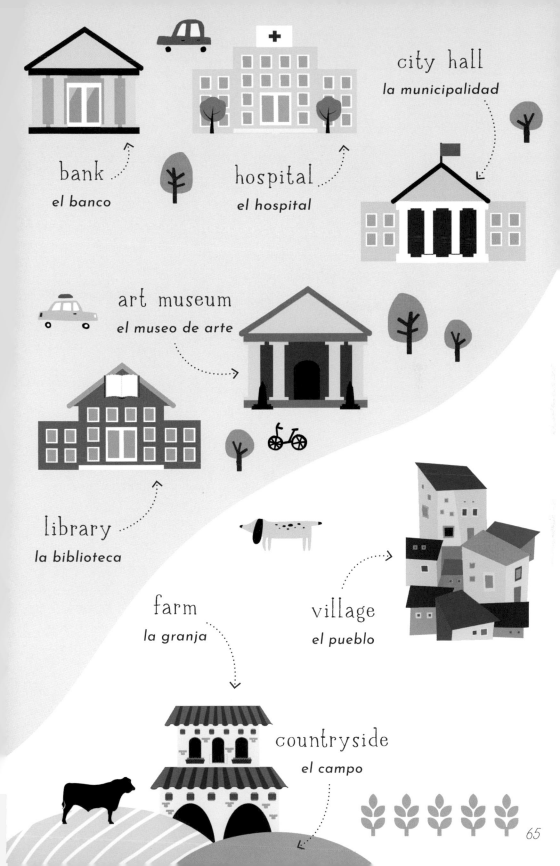

bank
el banco

hospital
el hospital

city hall
la municipalidad

art museum
el museo de arte

library
la biblioteca

farm
la granja

village
el pueblo

countryside
el campo

65

28

Construction

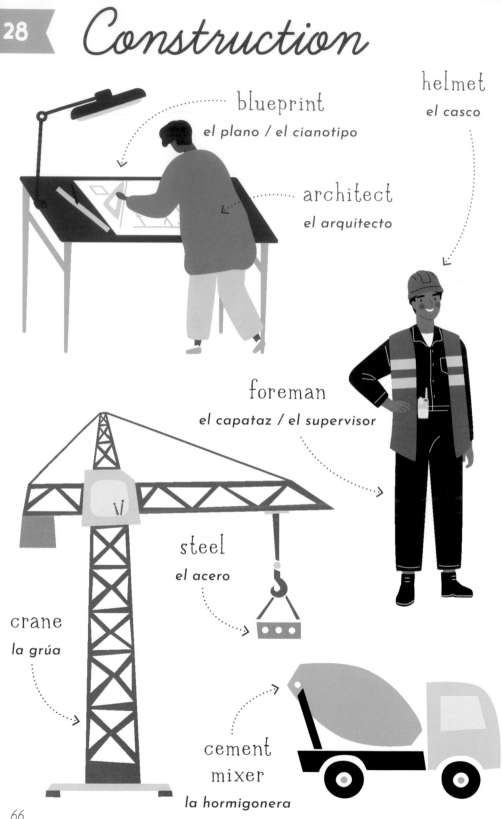

blueprint
el plano / el cianotipo

helmet
el casco

architect
el arquitecto

foreman
el capataz / el supervisor

steel
el acero

crane
la grúa

cement
mixer
la hormigonera

construction site
la obra / la zona de construcción / el sitio de construcción

glass
el vidrio

brick
el ladrillo

wood
la madera

worker
el obrero / el trabajador

bulldozer
la excavadora

dump truck
el volquete

29

Transportation

traffic
el tráfico

transportation
la transportación

In Chile they have communal cars called *colectivos* that up to four people can get into together!

bus stop
la parada /
la parada de
autobús

signal /
traffic light
el semáforo

street
la calle

bus
el autobús /
el bus

taxi
el taxi

car
el carro /
el coche /
el auto

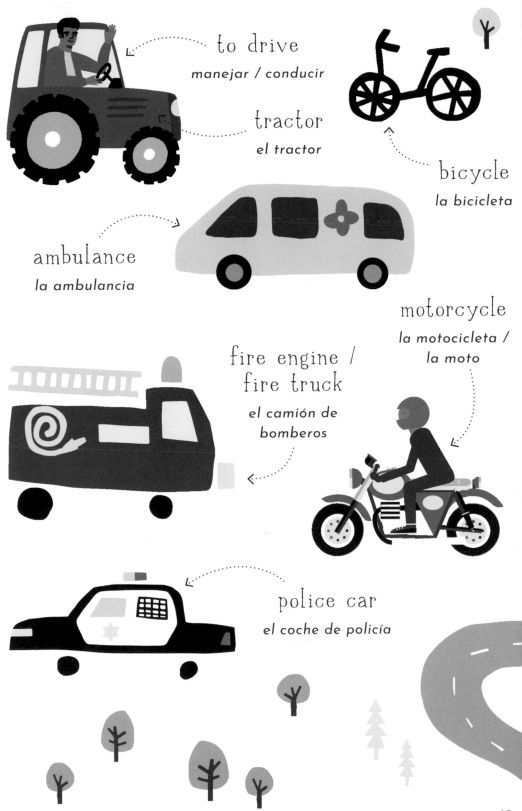

to drive
manejar / conducir

tractor
el tractor

bicycle
la bicicleta

ambulance
la ambulancia

motorcycle
la motocicleta /
la moto

fire engine /
fire truck
el camión de
bomberos

police car
el coche de policía

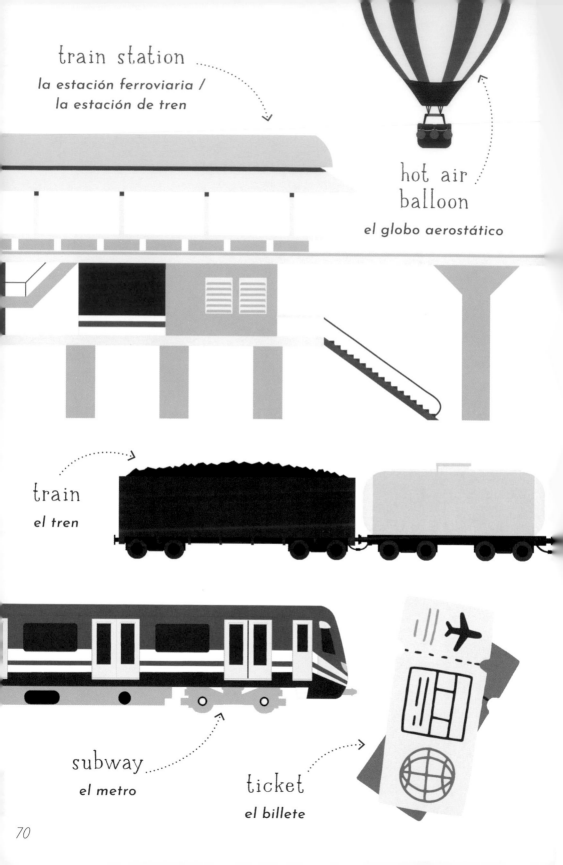

train station

*la estación ferroviaria /
la estación de tren*

**hot air
balloon**

el globo aerostático

train

el tren

subway

el metro

ticket

el billete

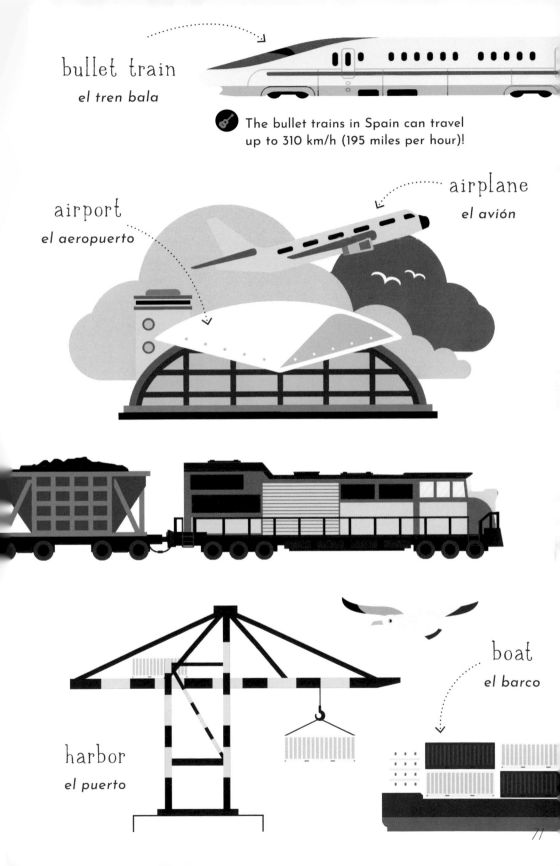

bullet train

el tren bala

The bullet trains in Spain can travel up to 310 km/h (195 miles per hour)!

airplane

el avión

airport

el aeropuerto

boat

el barco

harbor

el puerto

71

30

Travel

inn
la posada

trip /
journey
el viaje

vacation
las vacaciones

hotel room
la habitación del hotel

hotel
el hotel

passport
el pasaporte

overseas /
abroad
el extranjero

PASSPORT

Goodbye! We'll see each other again in two weeks.

¡Adiós! Nos veremos de vuelta en dos semanas.

travel agency
la agencia de viajes

luggage
el equipaje

to reserve
reservar

SALIDAS

departure
la salida / la partida

LLEGADAS

arrival
la llegada

31

Around Spanish-Speaking Cities

street vendor
el ambulante

Street vendors are very common and will often be found in places where a lot of cars pass by or where there is lots of foot traffic. Mexico City has a total of 121,738 street vendor stalls!

palace
el palacio

museum
el museo

One of the most famous museums in the world, the Prado (Museo Nacional del Prado), is found in Madrid, Spain. It houses priceless artwork from famous Spanish artists like Goya and Bosch.

Many Spanish cities have elaborate palaces built in European styles. The Government Palace (Palacio de Gobierno) in Lima, Peru, is the home of Peru's president. Lima's first Government Palace was built in 1535! But today's palace was constructed in the 1930s.

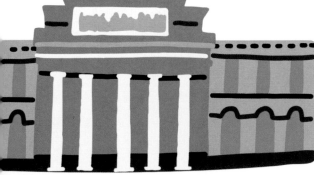

monument
el monumento

café
el café

garden
el jardín

🎸 The National Flag Memorial (Monumento Nacional a la Bandera) in Rosario, Argentina, is among the top twenty sites visited in South America.

🎸 The Catedral de Santa María la Menor in Santo Domingo, Dominican Republic, is over 450 years old and is the oldest cathedral in the Americas!

cathedral
la catedral

bridge
el puente

Museum

statue
la estatua

column
la columna

tourists
los turistas

gallery
la galería

dinosaur
el dinosaurio

skeleton
el esqueleto

exhibit
la exposición

artifact
el artefacto

tour guide
el guía turístico

fossil
el fósil

Shopping

shop
la tienda

store
la tienda

How much is it?
¿Cuánto cuesta?

money
el dinero

to buy
comprar

customer
el cliente

Spanish-speaking countries use different money, depending on the country. Pesos, euros, and dollars are some of the most common.

78

I often go to the bookstore to find good books.

Voy a la biblioteca con frecuencia para encontrar buenos libros.

cheap / inexpensive
barato

expensive
caro

convenience store
la tienda

supermarket
el supermercado

bookstore
la librería

bakery
la panadería

department store
los grandes almacenes / el centro comercial

34

Home

house
la casa

window
la ventana

chimney
la chimenea

roof
el techo

wall
la pared

apartments
los apartamentos

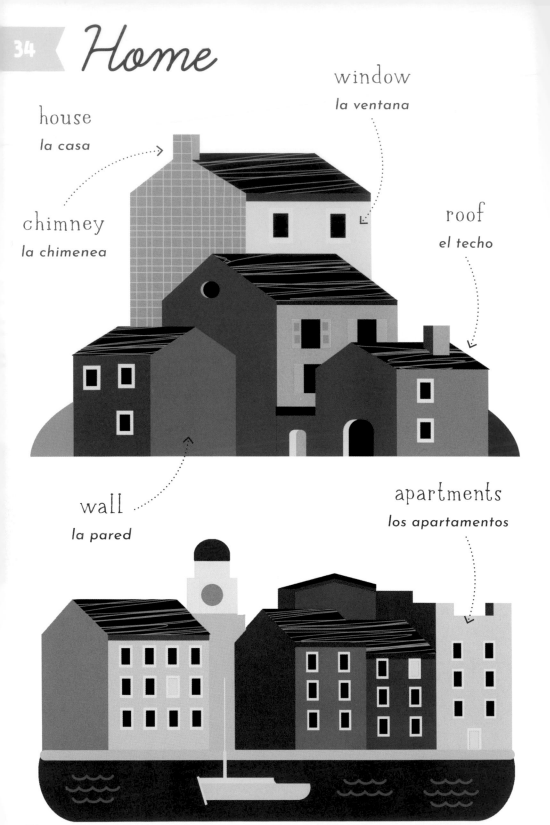

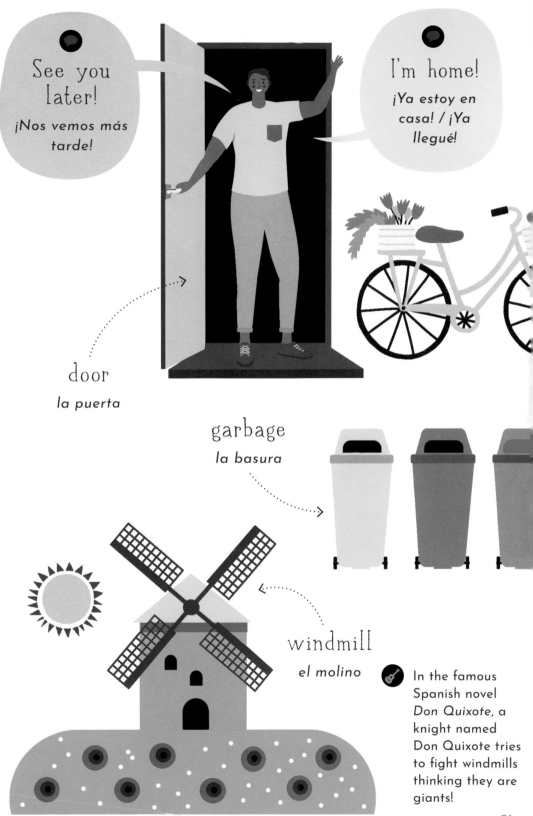

See you later!
¡Nos vemos más tarde!

I'm home!
¡Ya estoy en casa! / ¡Ya llegué!

door
la puerta

garbage
la basura

windmill
el molino

In the famous Spanish novel *Don Quixote*, a knight named Don Quixote tries to fight windmills thinking they are giants!

35

Bedroom

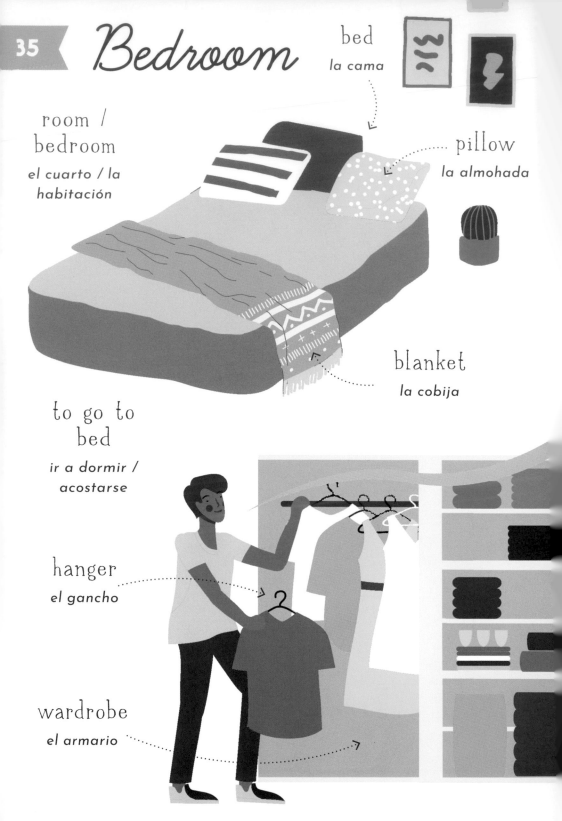

bed
la cama

room / bedroom
el cuarto / la habitación

pillow
la almohada

blanket
la cobija

to go to bed
ir a dormir / acostarse

hanger
el gancho

wardrobe
el armario

I have to clean my room.
Tengo que limpiar mi cuarto.

dark
oscuro

bright
brillante

light
la luz

to sleep
dormir

to awaken /
to wake up
despertarse

turn on
prender

turn off
apagar

mirror
el espejo

switch
el interruptor

83

Bathroom

to wash
lavar

to shower
ducharse

bathroom
el baño

bath
el baño / la bañera

toilet
*el inodoro /
el baño*

**to brush
(teeth)**
*cepillarse
(los dientes)*

● My little brother is learning to use the toilet.
Mi hermano menor está aprendiendo a usar el baño.

sink
el lavabo

Kitchen

kitchen
la cocina

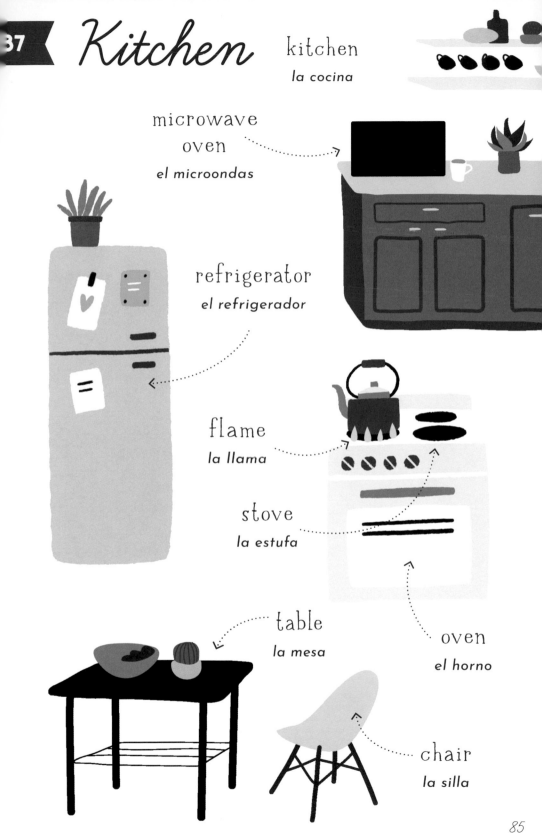

microwave oven
el microondas

refrigerator
el refrigerador

flame
la llama

stove
la estufa

oven
el horno

table
la mesa

chair
la silla

School

school
la escuela

kindergarten
**el kindergarten /
la guardería**

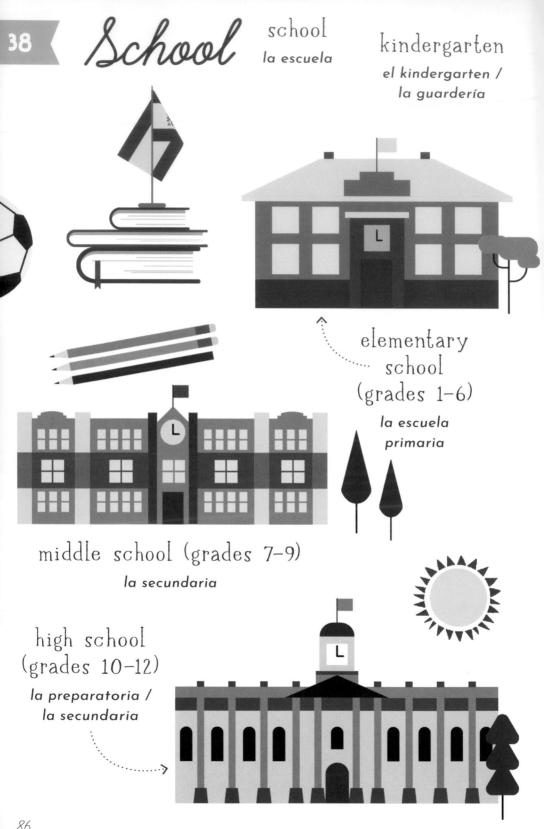

elementary
school
(grades 1–6)

**la escuela
primaria**

middle school (grades 7–9)

la secundaria

high school
(grades 10–12)

**la preparatoria /
la secundaria**

uniform /
school uniform

el uniforme / el uniforme escolar

teacher

el maestro / la maestra

student

el estudiante

In Spain, school lunches are sometimes served family-style from big bowls on the table.

university

la universidad

school lunch

el almuerzo escolar

39

Classroom

classroom
el aula / el salón de clase

💡 Careful! This word is feminine despite having *el* as the article.

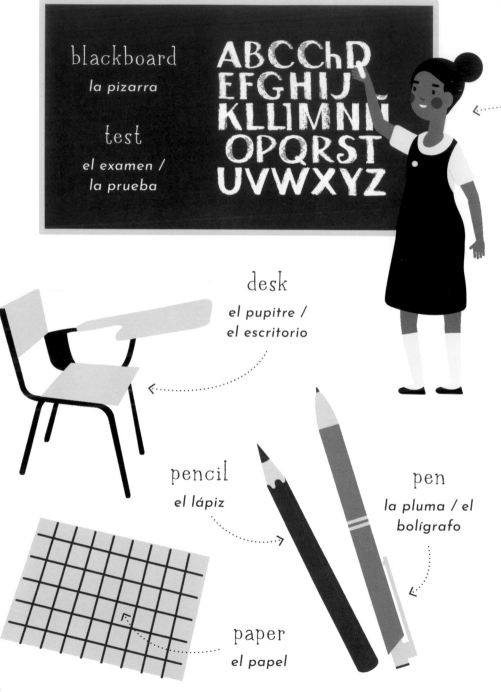

blackboard
la pizarra

test
el examen / la prueba

ABCChD EFGHIJ KLLlMNÑ OPQRST UVWXYZ

desk
el pupitre / el escritorio

pencil
el lápiz

pen
la pluma / el bolígrafo

paper
el papel

It's important to study well to pass the exam.

Es importante estudiar para pasar el examen.

to study
estudiar

to write
escribir

textbook
el manual / el libro de texto

book
el libro

schoolbag
la mochila

page
la página

homework
la tarea

Subjects

education
la educación

class
la clase / el curso

school
subject
*materia escolar
/ asignatura
escolar*

lesson
la lección

language
el idioma

mathemathics
las matemáticas

Spanish language
(school subject
for native
students)
El curso de español

English
(language)
*El curso de
inglés*

grammar
la gramática

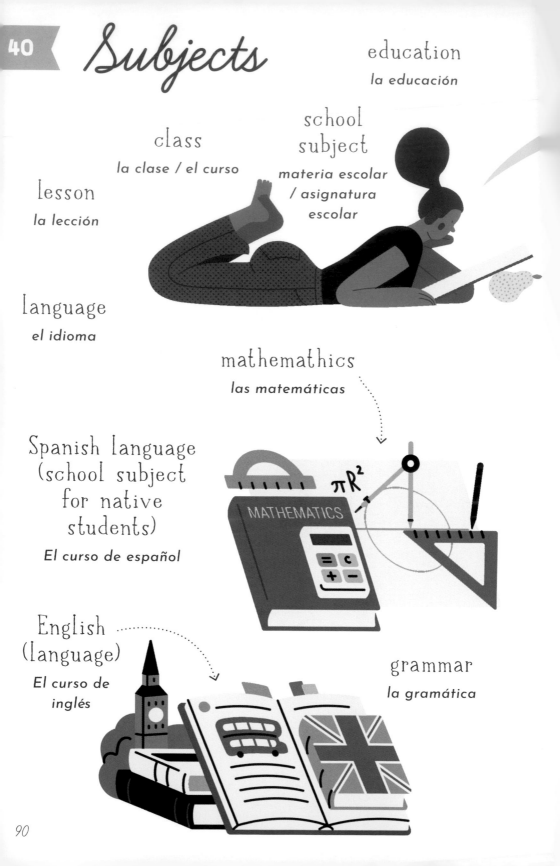

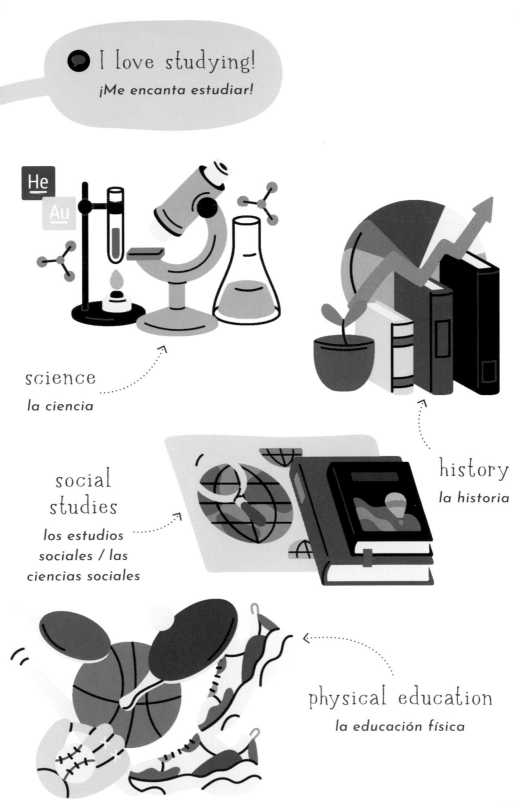

I love studying!

¡Me encanta estudiar!

science

la ciencia

history

la historia

social studies

los estudios sociales / las ciencias sociales

physical education

la educación física

Science

experiment
el experimento

scientist
el científico

hypothesis
la hipótesis

astronomy
la astronomía

physics
la física

laboratory
el laboratorio

chemistry
la química

to discover
descubrir

medical
equipment
el material médico

biology
la biología

geology
la geología

93

Learning

to learn
aprender

to teach
enseñar

word
la palabra

vocabulary
el vocabulario

question
la pregunta

correct
correcto

to understand
entender

to study
estudiar

to memorize
memorizar

to forget
olvidar

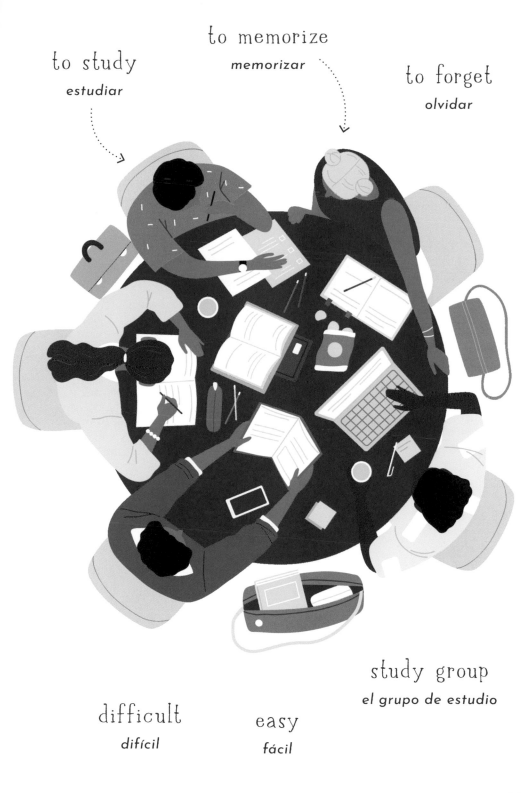

study group
el grupo de estudio

difficult
difícil

easy
fácil

43

Health

health
la salud

injury
la lesión

pain
el dolor

healthy
saludable

spirit
el espíritu

safe
seguro

illness
la enfermedad

bone
el hueso

headache
el dolor de cabeza

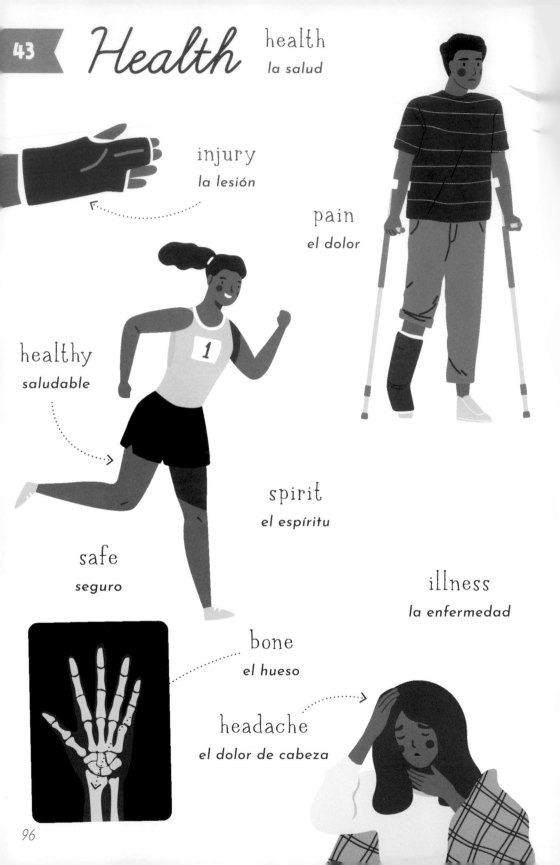

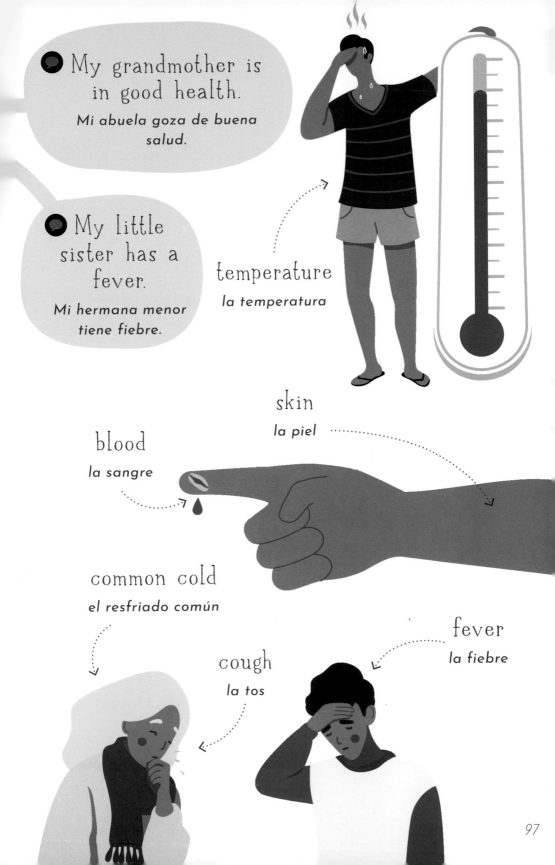

44

Work

to work
trabajar

part-time job
el trabajo a tiempo parcial

meeting room
la sala de reunión

company
la empresa / la compañía

office
la oficina

employee
el empleado / la empleada

I finally have free time! I will relax on the couch with my favorite book.

¡Por fin tengo tiempo libre! Me relajaré en el sofá con mi libro preferido.

to relax
relajarse

day off
el día libre

police officer
el policía

lawyer
la abogada / el abogado

nurse
la enfermera / el enfermero

doctor
la doctora / el doctor

45

Hobbies

to hike
escalar

hobby / pastime
la afición / el hobby / el pasatiempo

yarn
el hilo

to read
leer

to knit
tejer

movie theater
el cine

animation
la animación

movie
la película

game
el juego

fun
divertido

to play
jugar

to sing
cantar

voice
la voz

to dance
bailar

gardening
la jardinería

guitar
la guitarra

piano
el piano

Music

music
la música

composer
el compositor

harp
el arpa

🔆 Careful! This word is feminine despite having *el* as the article.

flute
la flauta

musician
el músico

saxophone
el saxofón

tambourine
la pandereta

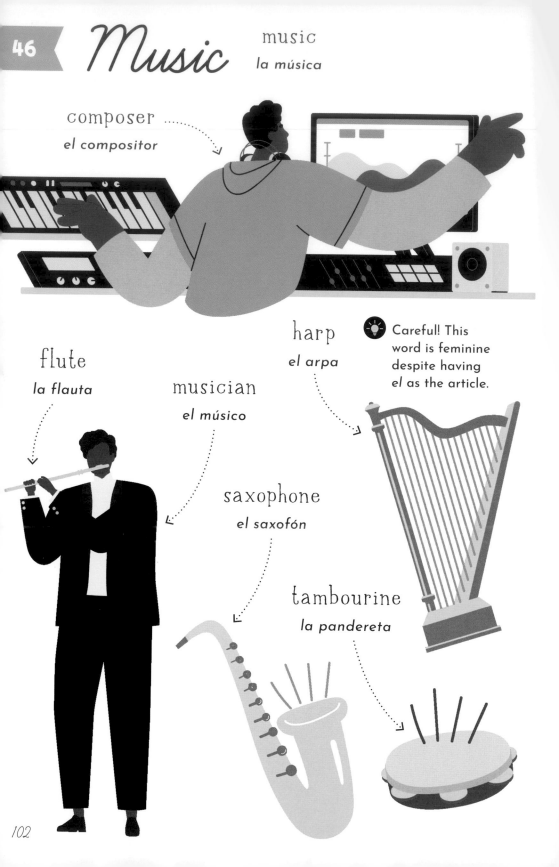

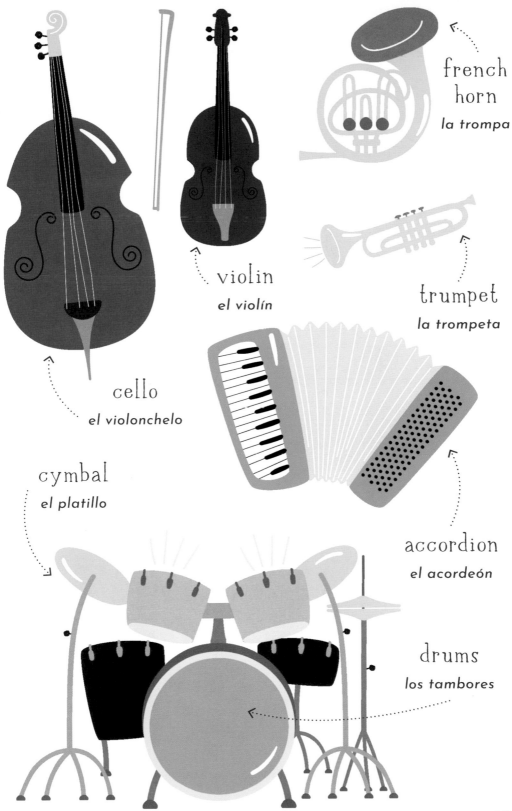

french
horn
la trompa

violin
el violín

trumpet
la trompeta

cello
el violonchelo

cymbal
el platillo

accordion
el acordeón

drums
los tambores

47

Art

potter
el alfarero /
el artesano

ceramics
la cerámica

easel
el caballete

painting
la pintura /
el cuadro

ink
la tinta

photography
la fotografía

charcoal
el carboncillo

pastel
el pastel

watercolor
la acuarela

brushes
los pinceles

oil paint
el óleo / la pintura al óleo

eraser
el borrador / la goma

model
el modelo

tape
la cinta

artist
el artista

Sports

sports
los deportes

basketball
el baloncesto / el básquetbol / el básquet

soccer
el fútbol

baseball
el béisbol

athlete
el atleta / el deportista

Soccer is certainly the most popular sport throughout Central and South America. Uruguay and Argentina are the only western Spanish-speaking countries to have won the World Cup with 2 victories for Uruguay and 3 for Argentina who are the current world champions! *¡Vamos Argentina!*

team
el equipo

victory
la victoria

defeat
la derrota

football
el fútbol americano

player
el jugador

to exercise
hacer ejercicio

to walk
caminar

to practice
practicar

to run
correr

ping pong / table tennis
el ping-pong / el tenis de mesa

match
el partido

tennis
el tenis

volleyball
el voleibol

swimming
la natación

49

Holidays

birthday
el cumpleaños

Easter
La Pascua

Day of the Dead
El Día de los Muertos

On Día de los Muertos, families create ofrendas or offerings with food and drink for their deceased ancestors so that they'll come back for a visit.

Mexican Independence Day
El Día de la Independencia de México

The Cry of Dolores or El Grito de Dolores takes place every year in Mexico City to commemorate the first cry in Dolores, Mexico, when a church bell was rung to give the call to arms that triggered the Mexican War of Independence.

Halloween
El Halloween / el Día de Brujas

🎸 On July 24, many Latin American nations celebrate Simón Bolívar's birthday. Bolívar helped several nations gain independence from Spain in the 1800s.

Mother's Day
El Día de la Madre

Father's Day
El Día del Padre

Simón Bolívar's Birthday
Natalicio de Simón Bolívar

Christmas Eve
La Nochebuena

Christmas
La Navidad

Valentine's Day
El Día de San Valentín

New Year's Day
El Año Nuevo

50

Communication

communication
la comunicación

to speak
hablar

to say
decir

cell phone
el celular

Hello?
¿Hola?

to make a phone
call
*hacer una llamada
telefónica*

telephone
el teléfono

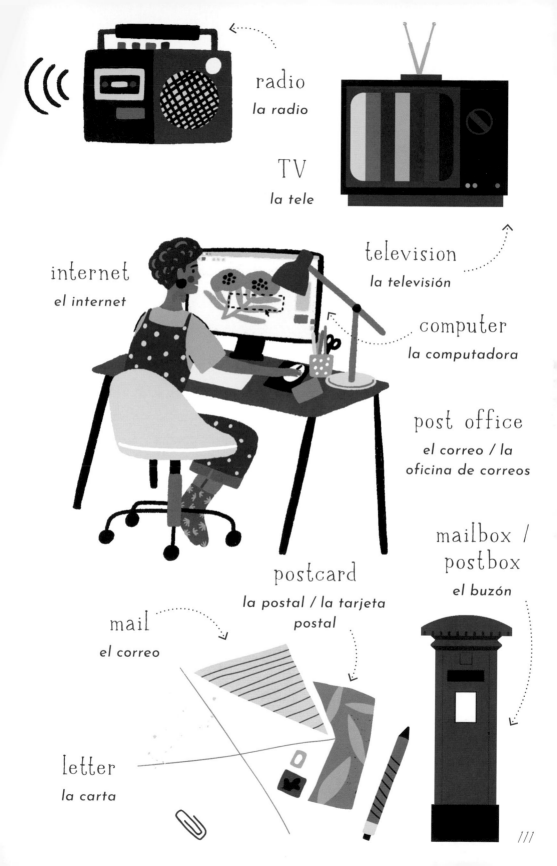

radio
la radio

TV
la tele

television
la televisión

internet
el internet

computer
la computadora

post office
el correo / la oficina de correos

mailbox / postbox
el buzón

postcard
la postal / la tarjeta postal

mail
el correo

letter
la carta

111

51

Fairy Tales

story
*la historia /
el cuento*

queen
la reina

once upon a time
érase una vez

king
el rey

tale
el cuento

castle
el castillo

prince
el príncipe

princess
la princesa

knight
el caballero

dragon
el dragón

cottage
la cabaña

witch
la bruja

legend
la leyenda

happily
ever after
*felices para
siempre*

wizard
el mago

Meals

meal
la comida

lunch
el almuerzo

breakfast
el desayuno

food
la comida

Generally speaking, in the Americas, people like to eat a lot of their food with just their hands!

dinner
la cena

dessert
el postre

to eat
comer

Drink

to drink
tomar / beber

tea
el té

hot chocolate
el chocolate caliente

milk
la leche

lemonade
la limonada

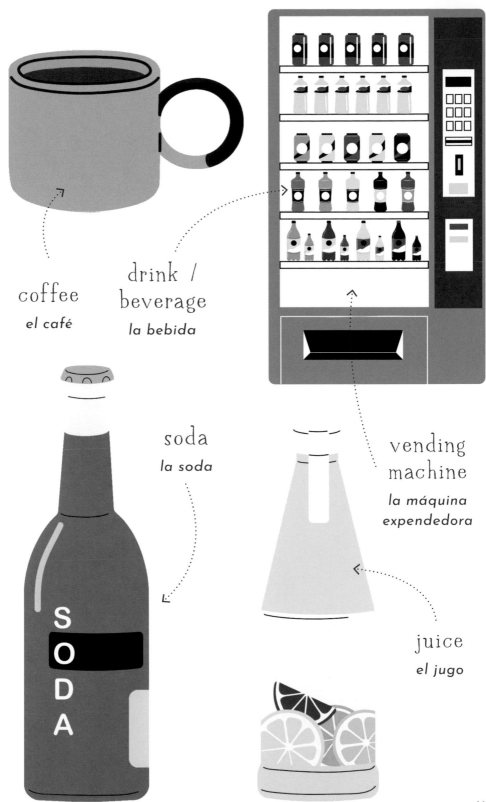

coffee
el café

drink /
beverage
la bebida

soda
la soda

vending
machine
*la máquina
expendedora*

juice
el jugo

Fruits

fruit
la fruta

apples
las manzanas

peach
el durazno

pear
la pera

orange
la naranja

pineapple
la piña

strawberry
la fresa

grape
la uva

fig
el higo

melon
el melón

watermelon
la sandía

banana
*el plátano /
la banana*

apricot
el albaricoque

Vegetables

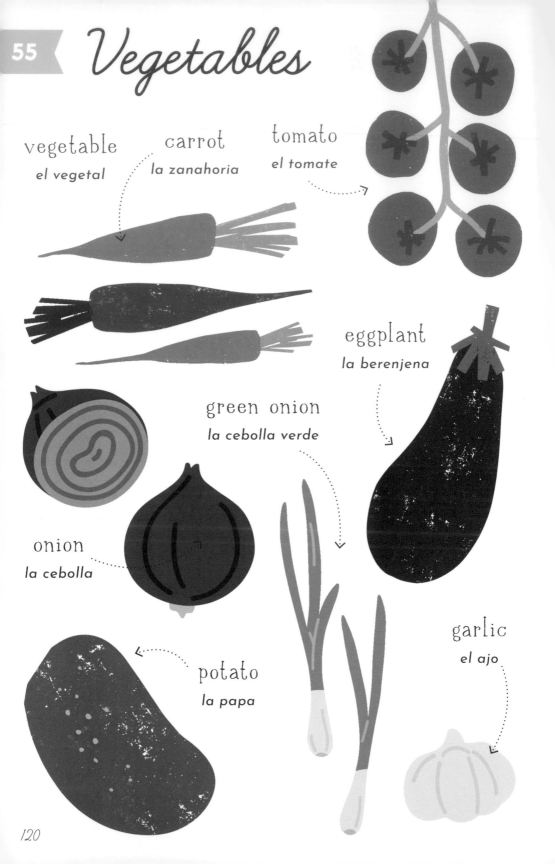

vegetable
el vegetal

carrot
la zanahoria

tomato
el tomate

eggplant
la berenjena

green onion
la cebolla verde

onion
la cebolla

potato
la papa

garlic
el ajo

broccoli
el brócoli

sweet potato
la batata / el camote

lettuce
la lechuga

celery
el apio

mushroom
el champiñón

cabbage
el repollo

121

56

Protein and Dairy

meat
la carne

beef
la carne de res

pork
la carne de cerdo

chicken (meat)
el pollo

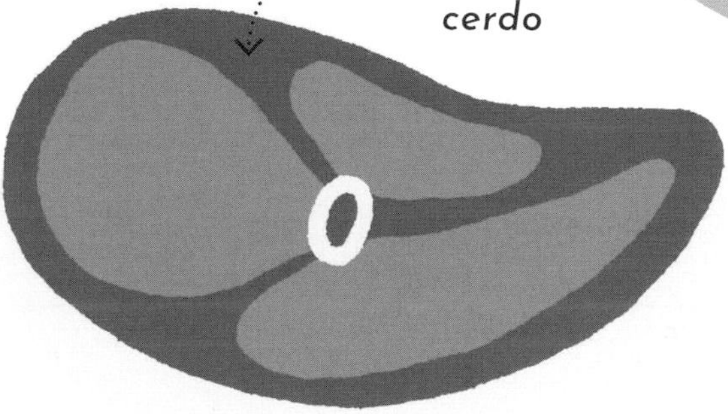

lobster
la langosta

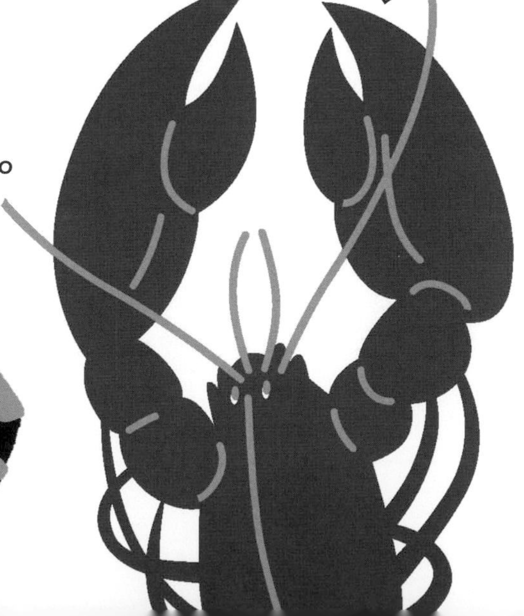

fish
el pescado

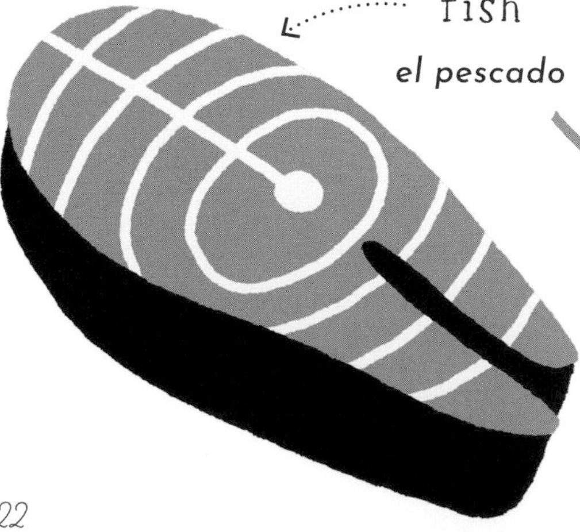

mussels
los mejillones

eggs
los huevos

butter
la mantequilla

dairy
products
*los productos
lácteos*

cheese
el queso

yogurt
el yogur

cream
la crema

57

Dessert

pastry

el bizcocho / la masa

sweet bread

el pan dulce

tres leches cake
(three-milk cake)

el pastel de tres leches

cookie

la galleta

chocolate

el chocolate

sweet

dulce

cake

el pastel / la torta

Refreshing! I love ice cream.

¡Refrescante! Me encanta la nieve.

In Mexico they will often call ice cream *nieve*, which also means "snow"!

ice cream
la nieve / el helado

tart
la tarta

churro
el churro

58

Cooking

to cook
cocinar

to bake
hornear

chef
el chef

Magnificent! This tastes very good.
¡Magnífico! Esto sabe muy rico.

flavor
el sabor

restaurant
el restaurante

ingredient
el ingrediente

cup
el vaso

sugar
el azúcar

knife
el cuchillo

fork
el tenedor

salt
la sal

spoon
la cuchara

pepper
la pimienta

recipe
la receta

frying pan / skillet
la sartén

dish towel
el trapo de cocina

saucepan / pot
la olla

cutting board
la tabla para cortar

59

Cuisine

 Made from a filling of meat and cheese grilled between corn dough, arepas are popular in Colombia, Panama, and Venezuela.

 A traditional soup flavored with green chiles, cumin, garlic, and lime, pozole is typically made with either chicken or pork and hominy. ¡Qué delicioso!

arepa
la arepa

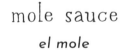

pozole soup
el pozole

 Mole is a sauce made from beef stock and thickened with dough made from corn flour.

mole sauce
el mole

rice
el arroz

 A famous dish from Spain, paella is cooked in a large pan called a *paellera*. Traditionally, the dish includes rice and a variety of seafood.

salsa
la salsa

ceviche
el ceviche

 Ceviche is made from raw fish cured in lemon or lime juice. It's eaten in many Latin American countries.

taco
el taco

 Tortillas have been around since the Aztecs, who called them *tlaxcalli*.

tortilla
la tortilla

paella
la paella

129

60

Numbers

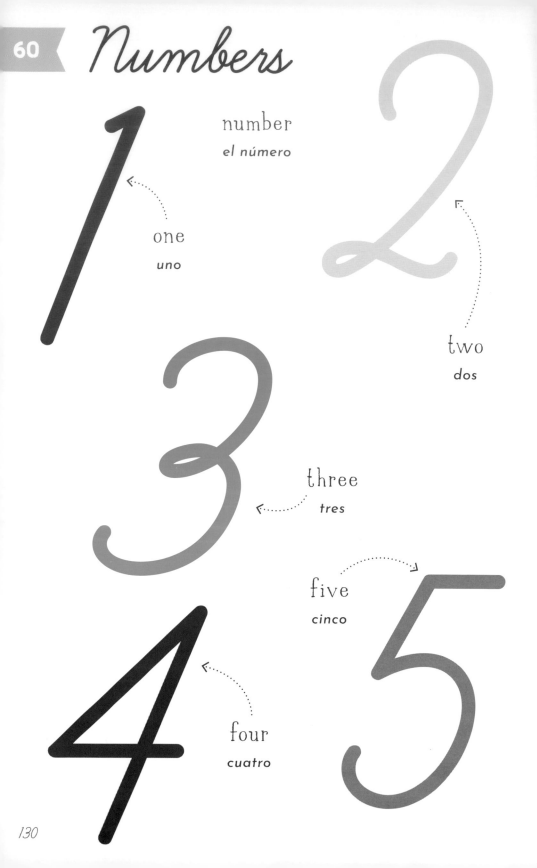

number
el número

1

one
uno

2

two
dos

3

three
tres

4

four
cuatro

5

five
cinco

6

six
seis

7

seven
siete

eight
ocho

8

nine
nueve

9

10

ten
diez

Bigger Numbers

11	eleven	once
12	twelve	doce
13	thirteen	trece
14	fourteen	catorce
15	fifteen	quince
16	sixteen	dieciséis
17	seventeen	diecisiete
18	eighteen	dieciocho
19	nineteen	diecinueve
20	twenty	veinte
30	thirty	treinta
40	forty	cuarenta
50	fifty	cincuenta
60	sixty	sesenta
70	seventy	setenta
80	eighty	ochenta
90	ninety	noventa
100	one hundred	cien
200	two hundred	doscientos
300	three hundred	trescientos
400	four hundred	cuatrocientos
500	five hundred	quinientos

600	six hundred	seiscientos
700	seven hundred	setecientos
800	eight hundred	ochocientos
900	nine hundred	novecientos
1,000	one thousand	mil
2,000	two thousand	dos mil
3,000	three thousand	tres mil
4,000	four thousand	cuatro mil
5,000	five thousand	cinco mil
6,000	six thousand	seis mil
7,000	seven thousand	siete mil
8,000	eight thousand	ocho mil
9,000	nine thousand	nueve mil
10,000	ten thousand	diez mil
20,000	twenty thousand	veinte mil
30,000	thirty thousand	treinta mil
40,000	forty thousand	cuarenta mil
50,000	fifty thousand	cincuenta mil
60,000	sixty thousand	sesenta mil
70,000	seventy thousand	setenta mil
80,000	eighty thousand	ochenta mil
90,000	ninety thousand	noventa mil

62

Making Numbers

As in English, large numbers in Spanish are just combinations of smaller numbers.

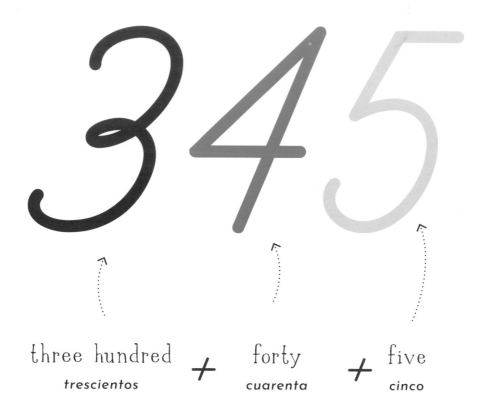

three hundred
trescientos

$+$

forty
cuarenta

$+$

five
cinco

three hundred forty-five
trescientos cuarenta y cinco

Here are some more examples. Can you see the same pattern here?

two thousand three hundred forty-five

dos mil trescientos cuarenta y cinco

twelve thousand three hundred forty-five

doce mil trescientos cuarenta y cinco

Word Index

nurse / 99
ocean / 26
octagon / 36
October / 55
office / 98
oil paint / 105
once upon a time / 112
one / 130
onion / 120
orange / 32
orange / 118
our / 23
oval / 37
oven / 85
overseas / abroad / 72
Pacific Ocean / 27
paella / 129
page / 89
pain / 96
painting / 104
palace / 74
Panama / 63
panda / 49
pants / 31
paper / 88
Paraguay / 63
parents / 38
parliament / 62
part-time job / 98
passport / 72
pastel / 104
pastry / 124
peach / 118
peak / 25
pear / 118
pen / 88
pencil / 88
penguin / 49
pentagon / 36
people / 21

pepper / 127
person / 20
Peru / 62
photography / 104
physical education / 91
physics / 92
piano / 101
pig / 48
pillow / 82
pineapple / 118
ping pong / table tennis / 107
pink / 33
plain / 24
planet / 42
plants / 46
player / 106
please / 18
polar bear / 49
police car / 69
police officer / 99
pork / 122
postcard / 111
post office / 111
pot / 47
potato / 120
potter / 104
pozole soup / 128
president / 63
prime minister / 62
prince / 112
princess / 112
Puerto Rico / 63
purple / 32
pyramid / 37
queen / 112
question / 94
radio / 111
rain / 45
rainbow / 45

raincoat / 31
really? / 19
recipe / 127
rectangle / 36
red / 32
refrigerator / 85
restaurant / 126
rice / 128
right / 41
river / 26
rock / boulder / 25
roof / 80
room / bedroom / 82
rose / 47
safe / 96
salmon / 51
salsa / 129
salt / 127
sand / 26
Saturday / 57
saucepan / pot / 127
saxophone / 102
scenery / landscape / 24
school / 86
schoolbag / 89
school lunch / 87
school subject / 90
science / 91
scientist / 92
sea / 26
season / 52
See you later! / 81
Senate / 62
September / 55
seven / 131
she / 23
shirt / 31
shoe / 31
shop / 78

short / 35
shoulder / 29
signal / traffic light / 68
silver / 33
Simón Bolívar's Birthday / 109
sink / 84
sisters / 39
six / 131
skeleton / 77
skin / 97
skirt / 31
sky / 43
small / 34
snake / 51
snow / 44
soccer / 106
social studies / 91
sock / 31
soda / 117
sometimes / 61
son / 38
south / 40
space / 42
Spain / 62
Spanish language (school subject for native students) / 90
sparrow / 50
sphere / 37
spirit / 96
spoon / 127
sports / 106
spring / 52
square / 36
star / 42
statue / 76
stature / height / 29
steel / 66
stomach / 29
stone / 25

store / 78
storm / 44
story / 112
stove / 85
strawberry / 119
street / 68
street vendor / 74
student / 87
study group / 95
suburb / 64
subway / 70
sugar / 127
suit / 30
summer / 52
sun / 43
Sunday / 57
supermarket / 79
sweet / 124
sweet bread / 124
sweet potato / 121
swimming / 107
switch / 83
table / 85
taco / 129
tale / 112
tall / 35
tambourine / 102
tape / 105
tart / 125
taxi / 68
tea / 116
teacher / 87
team / 106
telephone / 110
television / 111
temperature / 97
ten / 131
tennis / 107
test / 88
textbook / 89

thanks / 18
thank you very much / 18
that's right / 19
the four seasons / 52
their / 23
them / 23
the world / 24
they / 23
this month / 55
this week / 56
this year / 53
three / 130
thunder / 44
Thursday / 57
ticket / 70
to awaken / to wake up / 83
to bake / 126
to brush (teeth) / 84
to buy / 78
to cook / 126
to dance / 101
today / 61
toddler / 20
to discover / 93
to drink / 116
to drive / 69
to eat / 115
to exercise / 107
to forget / 95
to go to bed / 82
to hike / 100
toilet / 84
to knit / 100
to learn / 94
to make a phone call / 110
tomato / 120
to memorize / 95
tomorrow / 61
to play / 101

ABOUT THE AUTHOR

Tony Pesqueira lives near Houston, Texas. He is also the author of *My First Book of French*. His passions include being a husband and father to his wife and two sons, and all things soccer. Tony is fluent in English, Spanish, French, and Portuguese, and works as an interpreter and translator for these languages in the tech industry.

BUSHEL
& PECK
BOOKS

ABOUT BUSHEL & PECK BOOKS

Bushel & Peck Books is a children's publishing house with a special mission. Through our Book-for-Book Promise™, we donate one book to kids in need for every book we sell. Our beautiful books are given to kids through schools, libraries, local neighborhoods, shelters, nonprofits, and also to many selfless organizations that are working hard to make a difference. So thank you for purchasing this book! Because of you, another book will make its way into the hands of a child who needs it most.

NOMINATE A SCHOOL OR ORGANIZATION TO RECEIVE FREE BOOKS

Do you know a school, library, or organization that could use some free books for their kids? We'd love to help! Please fill out the nomination form on our website, and we'll do everything we can to make something happen.

www.bushelandpeckbooks.com/pages/
nominate-a-school-or-organization

If you liked this book, please leave a review online at your favorite retailer. Honest reviews spread the word about Bushel & Peck—and help us make better books, too!